C. M. Lathrop

Riverside recipe book

C. M. Lathrop

Riverside recipe book

ISBN/EAN: 9783337374839

Printed in Europe, USA, Canada, Australia, Japan

Cover: Foto ©Andreas Hilbeck / pixelio.de

More available books at **www.hansebooks.com**

RIVERSIDE RECIPE BOOK.

"We may live without poetry, music and art;
We may live without conscience and live without heart;
We may live without friends, we may live without books;
But civilized man cannot live without cooks."

—OWEN MEREDITH.

NEW YORK:
1890.

This Recipe Book has been compiled and edited in the interest of Christian Work in connection with the Rutgers Riverside Presbyterian Church.

Special attention is directed to the advertisements appearing in this volume, and it is hoped that the advertisers will receive the hearty support of all its readers.

CONTENTS.

SOUPS.

Soup Making	1	Tomato	5
General Stock	1	Pea	5
Beef	2	Turkey	6
Stock for Clear Soup	3	Tomato	6
Mutton	3	Cream of Celery	6
Green Corn	4	Okra	7
Mock Turtle	4	Clear Soup or Consommé	7
Black Bean	4	Clam	7
Bean	5	Green Pea	7

FISH.

Hints	9	Fish Chowder	11
Boiled Codfish	9	Oysters à la Poulette	11
Codfish Balls	10	Clam Fritters	12
Picked Codfish	10	Lobster Patties	12
Codfish Balls	10	Lobster a la Newburg	12
Warmed over Fish	11	Stewed Clams	13

MEATS.

Hash	15	Chopped Ham for Sandwiches	16
Chicken Croquettes	15	Cream Chicken	16
Mutton Stew	16	Corning Beef	17
A la Mode Beef	16	Spanish Beef	17

VEGETABLES.

Preparing Vegetables	19	Baked Beets	21
Delmonico Potatoes	20	Fried Potatoes with Cream Sauce	21
Corn Fritters	20		
Egg Plant	20	Green Corn Caked	21
Vegetable Oysters	20	Cooked Celery	21
Saratoga Potatoes	21	Potato Puff	22

ENTRÉES AND SALADS.

Potato Salad	23	Chicken Soufflé	26
Mayonnaise Dressing	23	A Nice Way to Cook Chicken	26
Cheese Soufflé	24	Broiled Sweetbreads	26
Chocolate Soufflé	24	Salad Dressing	27
Lobster Farcie	24	Chicken Salad	27
Purée of Salmon	25	To Roast Birds	27
Welsh Rare-bib	25	Bread Tarts	28
Hominy Croquette's	25	Sidney Smith's Salad Dressing	28

SAUCES.

Noodles for Soup	29	Celery Sauce	30
Bread Dice for Soup	29	Creamy Sauce	30
Poached Eggs for Consommé	29	Sauce Tartare	31
Egg Balls for Soup	30	Sauce for Plum or Fruit Pudding	31
Drawn Butter	30		

BREADS.

To cut Warm Bread	33	Pop Overs	35
Tip Top Rolls	33	Puffs for Breakfast	35
Corn Bread	33	Tea Cakes	35
Tea Rolls	34	Waffles	35
Muffins	34	Corn Bread	35
Puffetts	34	Corn Cake	36
Biscuits	34	Graham Muffins	36
Muffins	34	Gems	36

DESSERTS.

Weights and Measures	37	Wine Jelly	40
Velvet Cream	37	Indian Pudding	40
Lemon Cream	38	Pie Pastry	40
Cream Pie	38	Lemon and Raisin Pie	40
Huckleberry Pudding	38	Fig Pudding	41
Cold Cream Pudding	39	Lemon Pudding	41
Ambrosia	39	Orange Baskets	41
Coffee Jelly	39	Raspberry Joy	42
Caramel Custard	39		

CAKE.

General Directions	43	Sponge Cake Mrs. H—	46
Delicate Cake	44	Orange Cake Mrs. K—	46
Angel Cake	44	Pearl Cake	47
Coffee Cake	44	Ginger Cake	47
Helen Cake	45	Jumbles	47
Crullers	45	Fig Cake	47
Orange Cake	45	Sponge Cake Mrs. L—	48
Molasses Cake	45	Bread Cake	48

CANDIES.

Without Cooking.

French Creams	49	Cream Dates	50
French Vanilla Creams	49	Wintergreen Creams	50
English Walnut Creams	50	Peppermint Creams	50
Cream Cherries	50	Maple Sugar Creams	51

CANDIES.

Cooked.

Molasses Taffy	53	Chocolate Creams	54
Pea-nut Candy	53	Butter Scotch	55
Chocolate Caramels	53	Pea-nut Candy	55
Molasses Candy	54	Pop Corn Balls	55
Everton Taffy	54		

HINTS FOR THE SICK.

Beef Tea	58	Koumys Miss H—	60
Chicken Broth	58	For Catarrh	60
Mutton Broth	58	Rheumatism or any Pain	60
Oatmeal Gruel	58	Throat Gargle	60
Lemonade	58	Tonic	60
Flaxseed Tea	59	Cough Mixture	61
Cure for a Felon	59	Hoarseness	61
To Check a Cold	59	Excellent Tonic	61
Koumys Mrs. H—	59	Chalk Mixture	61

ODDS AND ENDS.

For Cleaning Brass	63	Remove Ink from Carpets	64
Baking Custard	63	To Polish Furniture	64
Tooth Powder	63	Poetical Appetizer	65
To Freshen Black Lace	63	Advertisements	67
Celery	64		

SOUPS.

"A hasty plate of soup."

Soup Making.

It can be made from the merest scraps and trimmings of meat, from the heads, tails and feet of animals; from the bones and skin of fish, from cereals and vegetables alone. Pot liquor in which meat has been boiled should always be saved and used for soup the next day, when by the removal of all fat, by careful skimming, and the addition of a few vegetables or some dumplings, rice, or macaroni, it will make a palatable broth. Experiments made by French chemists prove that the delicacy and richness of soup may be increased by first soaking the meat in tepid water enough to cover it, and adding this to the second water in which the meat is put over the fire, just as it reaches the boiling point.

General Stock.

Part I. Where there is a family of any size it is well to keep a clean pot or saucepan on the back of the stove to receive all clean scraps of meat, bones, and remains of poultry and game, which are found in every kitchen; but vegetables should not be put into it, as they are apt to sour. The proper proportions for soups are one pound of meat and bone to one and one-half quarts of cold water; the meat and bones to be well chopped and broken up, and put over the fire in cold water, being brought slowly to a boil, and carefully skimmed as often as scum rises, and being maintained at a steady boiling point from two to six hours, as time permits ; one hour before stock is done, add to it one carrot, and one turnip pared ; one onion, stuck with three cloves, and a bouquet of sweet herbs.

Part II. When the soup is to be boiled six hours, two quarts of cold water must be allowed to every pound of meat; this will be reduced to one quart in boiling ; two gills of soup are generally allowed for each person at table, when it is served as the first part of the dinner and meats are to follow it. Care should be taken that the stock-pot boils slowly and constantly, from one side, as rapid and irregular boiling clouds and darkens the stock as much as imperfect skimming. Stock should never be allowed to cool in the stock-pot, but should be strained into an earthen jar, and left standing to cool uncovered, and all the fat removed, and saved to clarify for drippings; the stock is then ready to heat and use for soup or gravy. When stock has been darkened and clouded by careless skimming and fast boiling, it can be clarified by adding to it one egg and the shell, mixed first with a gill of cold water, then with a gill of boiling soup, and stirring it briskly into the soup until it boils ; then remove it to the back of the fire, where it will not boil, and let it stand until the white and shell have collected the small particles clouding the soup ; then strain it once or twice, until it looks clear.

Beef Soup.

Take a shank of beef with plenty of meat upon it, and boil five or six hours the day before using. The next day skim off the grease, put the jelly in the soup kettle, and one hour before serving, add turnips, carrots, onions, and cabbage chopped fine in quantity desired; a few tomatoes and a little celery improve it. Season with pepper and salt. Drop in a few noodles. Three tablespoonsful of rice may be added with the vegetables.

Margery Daw in the Kitchen.

Stock for Clear Soup.

Four pounds of the middle cut of a shin of beef, remove the marrow from the bone; cut the meat into small pieces, put the meat and bone into a soup pot, with five quarts of cold water; put it on the hottest part of the fire, and allow it to boil up quickly, when it boils skim very carefully; throw in half a tablespoonful of salt, which brings the scum to the top again, remove this, and put in a small piece of turnip and carrot, half a root of celery, half a teaspoon of whole cloves, one onion (which must soak in boiling water ten minutes) and pepper; draw it to one side, and let it slowly simmer for five hours, strain through a seive before putting away; when cold, remove the fat on top of it.

Take one quart of stock, put it in a saucepan and heat it, break into a bowl two eggs, one tablespoonful of cold water, a little salt and pepper : when stock is hot, pour in the eggs and water ; and whisk it until it boils, put on the lid and allow it to simmer twenty minutes; pour it through a clean towel, and it is ready for use.

Eclectic Cook Book.

Mutton Soup.

Boil a leg of mutton three hours, and take the water for the soup, season with pepper and salt. Add a small cup of barley or rice, as preferred, throw in a little chopped parsley, if liked, and boil about an hour.

Margery Daw in the Kitchen.

Green Corn Soup.

Take one dozen ears of corn, scrape the cobs and boil them twenty minutes in one quart of water. Remove the cobs, put in the corn, and boil fifteen minutes. Add two quarts of rich milk seasoned with salt, pepper and butter, and thicken with two tablespoonsful of flour. Boil ten minutes and turn into a tureen in which are the well-beaten yolks of three eggs.

Margery Daw in the Kitchen.

Mock Turtle Soup.

One quart of black beans and five pounds of lean beef. Put into the soup kettle in the morning in cold water sufficient for the quantity of soup desired, and cook slowly all day. Strain through a seive. Add salt, pepper, and plenty of cloves, to taste. Let it stand all night. When desired to serve, cut two lemons into thin slices, put them into the tureen and pour over them the soup.

Margery Daw in the Kitchen.

Black Bean Soup.

One quart of black beans, one pound of lean beef, one half pound salt pork, three quarts of water. Soak the beans all night, and in the morning pour off the water and put them in the soup kettle, with three quarts of cold water, in which are the meat and pork. Boil three or four hours, adding water as it boils away. Slice some lemon into the tureen before serving, also some bread cut into small pieces, and fried in butter. Strain through a colander into the tureen.

Margery Daw in the Kitchen.

Bean Soup.

Soak one quart of beans over night in cold water, in the morning pour off the water, and put them in a kettle with four quarts of water, boil until soft enough to pass through the colander. Season with pepper and salt, and a piece of butter the size of an egg, or boil with the beans a piece of salt pork. Throw pieces of bread cut into small pieces and fried in butter into the tureen, and strain the soup upon them; if the soup is too thick, add boiling water.

Margery Daw in the Kitchen.

Tomato Soup.

One and one-half pounds of lean beef in one gallon of water boiled down to three pints, add one quart of tomatoes, one cup of sweet milk, two tablepoonfuls of flour rubbed into a piece of butter the size of an egg. Then boil one hour, but less will do. Season with pepper and salt, and strain through a colander.

Margery Daw in the Kitchen.

Pea Soup.

One quart of split peas soaked overnight in two quarts of water. In the morning pour off the water and put the peas in the soup kettle with four quarts of water. Let them boil until cooked enough to pass through the colander; about two hours. As soon as it begins to boil, cut up one large onion and fry brown in a spider with a piece of butter the size of a large egg, and put into the kettle with the soup. Strain, and season with salt and pepper before serving. As the water boils away add more. A couple of slices of salt pork or a little beef stock is a great improvement.

Margery Daw in the Kitchen.

Turkey Soup.

Place the frame of the cold turkey, with the remnants of dressing and gravy in a pot, and cover with cold water, simmer gently three hours, let it stand until the next day. Remove the fat, and skim off the bits and bones. Put the soup on to heat until it boils; then thicken with flour slightly wet with water, and season to taste.

Margery Daw in the Kitchen.

Tomato Soup.

One pound of meat, two quarts of water, boil away to three pints, then add a tea cup of milk, a lump of butter size of an egg rubbed in two tablespoons of sifted flour, and one quart of stewed tomatoes, salt, and boil an hour after everything is in.

Cream of Celery Soup.

Take the white part of two large heads of celery, either grate it or chop it very fine, boil in a quart of milk, with one cup of rice, allow the rice and celery to stew slowly, until they can be rubbed through a coarse sieve, adding more milk if it gets too thick, then add to it an equal quantity of strong veal or chicken stock, white pepper and salt to taste.

Eclectic Cook Book.

Okra Soup.

To one quart of stock add two chopped onions, four tomatoes and eight okra sliced thin, a small carrot grated; pepper and salt to taste. To make a quart of soup allow three pints of stock; vegetables require boiling an hour, sometimes even longer.

Mrs. F. E. Lathrop.

Clear Soup or Consommé.

(Two quarts for eight persons). This is made by straining two quarts of stock, which has been cooled and freed from fat through a piece of flannel or a napkin, until it is bright and clear; if this does not entirely clear it, use an egg, as directed for clarifying soup, then season it to taste with salt, using at first a teaspoonful, and a very little fine white pepper, say a quarter of a saltspoonful, and color it to a bright straw color with caramel, of which a scant teaspoonful will be about the proper quantity.

Clam Soup.

Wash fifty clams, put them in a pot and cover them with water, let them boil, and as soon as the shells open take them out with a skimmer.

Chop the clams, strain the water they were boiled in, and return to the kettle, add the chopped clams, one quart of milk, pepper and salt (not much), one-fourth pound of butter, and thicken with rolled cracker.

Green Pea Soup.

One pint of stock, one can of peas, a piece of onion, size of a small nutmeg. Boil together half an hour, strain, and put in soup-pot again, with one pint of milk. Let it come to a boil; season with salt and pepper, and stir in one tablespoonful of butter. Add one teaspoonful of parsley, chopped fine.

Mrs. Walton.

FISH.

"Now, good digestion waits on appetite, health on both, and a waiter on all three."

Hints.

Nearly all kinds of fish lose their flavor soon after they are taken from the water.

Fish are fresh when the eyes are clear, the fins stiff, the gills red and hard to open.

Before broiling fish, rub the gridiron with fat to keep it from sticking. Place the inside of the fish down on the gridiron, and nearly cook before turning; butter the skin before turning towards the fire.

Salt fish should be soaked in cold water over night before cooking.

Boiled Codfish.

Lay the fish in cold water, slightly salted, for half an hour before it is time to cook it, wipe dry and put in a fish kettle with water enough to cover it, in which has been dissolved a little salt. Let it boil quite briskly. A piece of cod weighing three pounds will be cooked in half an hour from the time the water begins to boil. If cooked in a cloth it will require twice as long to boil.

Have ready a sauce prepared thus: To one gill of boiling water add as much milk, and when it is scalding hot stir in two tablespoonsful of butter, a little at a time, that it may melt without oiling, a tablespoonful of flour wet with cold water, and as this thickens, two beaten eggs. Season with salt and chopped parsley, and after one good boil take from the fire and add a dozen capers. Put the fish into a hot dish and pour sauce over it.

Codfish Balls.

One coffee-cup of codfish, very finely shreded, eight good sized potatoes. Pour boiling water on both together, boil twenty-five minutes. Mash with fork, then add one tablespoonful of butter, one egg. Form into balls, and drop into boiling fat for one minute.

Picked up Codfish.

Put fish on the stove in cold water; keep warm, but do not boil until the fish is softened; remove bones and skin, shred finely, and put in a saucepan, with rich milk in proportion of one pint of milk to one cup of fish; let it come to a boil and thicken with a teaspoonful of flour.

Just before taking from the stove, stir in butter the size of an egg, and one egg well beaten. Season with pepper and garnish with hard boiled eggs.

The Ideal Cook Book.

Codfish Balls.

One pound of codfish picked fine, two pints raw potatoes cut in small pieces. Boil together in a little water. When done soft, drain and mash; add three eggs, half a cup of butter, and pepper to taste. Make into balls, and fry in hot lard.

The Ideal Cook Book.

Warming over Fish.

Pick it up finely, mix with drawn butter, line the bottom and sides of a pudding dish with mashed potatoes, so that it stands up above the edge, pour the fish into the hollow, brown all in the oven, and garnish with hard boiled eggs.

Eclectic Cook Book.

Fish Chowder.

Take four slices of salt pork and fry brown in the bottom of the pot, and pour off the grease, chop the pork fine. Put in the bottom of the pot a layer of haddock or fresh cod, any other firm fish will do, cut in thin slices; next a layer of crackers with some of the chopped pork and thin slices of onion, then fish, and so on until the whole is used. Season with pepper and salt ; pour over hot water enough to cover well, and boil one hour. Serve hot as soup.

Oysters á la Poulette.

Put a solid quart of oysters on the stove to boil in their own liquor. As soon as they begin to boil, skim carefully, and turn into a strainer, and when they have been well drained set them aside. Put half a pint of oyster liquor into a saucepan, and when it begins to boil, stir into it one heaping teaspoonful of flour mixed with three tablespoonsful of cold water. Boil gently five minutes longer. Put a pint of cream into a double boiler, and when it begins to boil, add the thickened oyster liquor. Season with salt and pepper, a slight grating of nutmeg, and a grain of cayenne. Have at hand the yolks of four eggs, well beaten, and add to them half a cupful of cold cream. Now add to the cooking mixture the oysters, a tablespoonful of butter, and finally the egg mixture. Cook for three minutes, stirring all the time ; then remove from the fire immediately, and serve.

Miss Parloa.

Clam Fritters.

Two dozen clams chopped. Stir into them three well beaten eggs and three tablespoonsful of their own liquor; add flour enough to make a thin batter; fry in a spider in hot butter and lard. When brown on one side, turn the other side.

Margery Daw in the Kitchen.

Lobster à la Newburg.

Three quarters of a pound of lobster, for seven or eight people, one claret glass of sherry wine, one cup of cream, the yolk of one egg. Put butter in pan, then the lobster, sherry, pepper and salt. Let it come to a boil. Take the cream with the egg, and let it come to a boil ; then put lobster in a dish and pour cream over it.

Mrs. W. H. Beadleston.

Lobster Patties.

One pint of lobster cut into dice, half a pint of white sauce, a speck of cayenne, one eighth of a teaspoonful of mustard; heat all together, fill the shell and serve.

Miss Parloa.

Salmon or any kind of fish may be used in the same way.

Stewed Clams.

Take the clams from the shells, as many as you wish, put them into a stew pan with their own liquor, butter and pepper. Let them stew slowly. Butter some slices of toast, and pour them over. Serve in a deep dish.

MEATS.

"Hunger is the best seasoning for meats."
CICERO.

Hash.

Melt a piece of butter (the size of an egg) in a pan, stir in one teaspoonful of flour until smooth, add one cupful of milk, stir slowly until it boils, then add one and one-half cupful of meat and one cupful of potatoes; let the hash boil five or ten minutes, then put it in the dish and brown in the oven.

Chicken Croquettes.

Two large cups of chicken chopped very fine, take a piece of butter the size of an egg, and one large spoon of flour and melt them together, then add one large cup of the water the chicken was boiled in, and one half teacup of milk; cook this to consistency of drawn butter, then add one coffee cup of bread crumbs, season with salt and pepper, then add the chicken, and cook slowly for a few minutes. When done, spread on a dish to cool, then make into form, dip them in beaten egg, then roll them in crackers crumbs and fry in boiling lard; this rule makes twelve. Veal can be substituted for chicken.

Mrs. T. F. Sharpe.

Mutton Stew.

Take slices of cold boiled mutton, put in the stew pan one teaspoonful mustard, two teaspoonsful of currant jelly, a piece of butter, size of a walnut, nearly a teacup of catsup, cook ten minutes, and then put in the meat, and cook until it is thoroughly hot.

Mrs. T. F. Sharpe.

A la Mode Beef.

Take a round of beef, cut five or six gashes in it, and put in your dressing which is seasoned with cloves, nutmeg, pepper, salt and butter. Then sew up the gashes, tie it up in a cloth and boil it two hours, then put it in the oven and let it brown over. Boil the water in the pot down to a thick gravy.

Mrs. F. E. Lathrop.

Chopped Ham for Sandwiches.

Two pounds of boiled ham chopped fine, one pound of butter, one tablespoon of mustard, two tablespoon of Worcestershire sauce, one teacup of cream. Beat all the ingredients together, until they become a smooth paste. Then spread between bread without otherwise putting butter on, that being prepared with the ham is sufficient.

Mrs. S. S. Stewart.

Cream Chicken.

Take young tender chickens and cut them up as for fricasse, wash them well and dry in a towel, salt the pieces, and dip each one in flour.

Put nice, clean lard in the frying pan, and when hot lay in the chicken and fry slowly, turning the pieces over often, frying them brown. It generally takes an hour to get them well done, then take the chicken up, piece by piece, and put on the platter, then strain the fat into a clean frying pan, having it free from all specks, and add a tea cup of milk and a piece of butter, mix a tablespoonful of flour in a little milk, very smooth, and stir in when it boils. This gravy may be poured over the chicken, or put in a gravy dish, as you prefer, it must be very white, not thick; chopped parsley may be added to the gravy.

Mrs R. R. Booth.

Corning Beef.

Cut and pack the beef in barrel. For one hundred pounds take six pounds of salt, two ounces of saltpetre, one cup of molasses (or one-half pound of sugar), put them in sufficient water to cover the beef. Boil the brine, and skim until clear, and pour over the beef while scalding hot. After one week it will be ready for use.

Spanish Beef.

Steam three or four pounds of round beef in water (cover tight) for three hours, one hour before done put in stewed or canned tomatoes, also one onion. Thicken after taking off. Very nice cold.

Mrs. J. E. Duryée.

VEGETABLES.

"Cheerful looks make every dish a feast."—MASSINGER.

Preparing Vegetables.

Always have them as fresh as possible; summer vegetables should be cooked on the same day they are gathered.

Look them over, and wash well, cutting out all decayed or unripe parts.

Lay them, when peeled, in cold water for some time before using.

Always let the water boil before putting them in, and continue to boil until done.

TURNIPS.—Should be peeled, and boil from forty minutes to an hour.

BEETS.—Boil from one to two hours, then put in cold water and remove the skin.

PARSNIPS.—Boil twenty to thirty minutes.

SPINACH.—Boil twenty minutes, then rub through a colander.

ONIONS.—Boil in one, two or three waters; add a little milk the last time.

STRING BEANS.—Boil one hour.

LIMA BEANS.—Boil from half an hour to one hour.

GREEN CORN.—Boil thirty minutes.

GREEN PEAS.—Should be boiled in as little water as possible; boil twenty minutes.

ASPARAGUS.—Same as peas; serve on toast.

CABBAGE.—Should be boiled from one-half hour to one hour in plenty of water; salt while boiling.

Eclectic Cook Book.

Delmonico Potatoes.

Fill a pudding dish with stewed potatoes, grate some cheese over the top, and set it in the oven to brown over.

Corn Fritters.

One dozen ears of corn grated, one tablespoonful melted butter, one tablespoonful sweet milk, one-half teacupful flour, two eggs, little salt; fry.

Egg Plant.

Slice thin; sprinkle each slice with salt, pack together again, and let remain one hour; drain the water off, dip in egg, then in rolled cracker, and fry in hot butter or lard.

Vegetable Oysters.

Wash and scrape them well, cut into small round pieces, boil them an hour until tender, in sufficient water to cover them thoroughly. Pour off the whole, or a part of the water, as desired, add cream or milk. Season well with butter, pepper and salt, and if desired, thicken with flour, well mixed with cold water.

Margery Daw in the Kitchen.

Saratoga Potatoes.

Slice raw potatoes very thin, and let them stand several hours in ice water. Then dry them in a napkin, and fry in hot lard, and salt them.

Baked Beets.

Use beets uniform in size, wash and prepare the same as potatoes for baking; bake four hours, then peel and cut up as if boiled, and season to taste.

Mrs. J. J. Halpin.

Fried Potatoes with Cream Sauce.

Cut raw potatoes into balls or triangles, fry in hot lard, and pour over them cream, which has been heated, and slightly thickened if necessary. Season the cream with a little salt and white pepper.

Eclectic Cook Book.

Green Corn Cakes.

Six ears of corn grated, the yolks of two eggs, a little salt, three rolled crackers. Grease the griddle, drop from the spoon, and bake twenty minutes.

Margery Daw in the Kitchen.

Cooked Celery.

Cut the celery into pieces half an inch long, throw them into boiling water with a little salt, and boil three-quarters of an hour ; drain off the water and pour on cream if you have it, if not, milk enough to cover it. Season with butter, pepper, and salt to taste. It is not necessary to use the choicest pieces of celery.

Margery Daw in the Kitchen.

Potato Puff.

Boil the potatoes in salted water, drain off the water, and dry them a few minutes. Mash them perfectly smooth. To a pint of mashed potato put two tablespoonsful of butter, and beat with a large fork, until light and creamy; add the yolks of two eggs, a small cup of rich milk, and lastly the whites of two eggs beaten to a froth. Beat each ingredient in before adding the next. Add more salt if needed; put in a buttered baking dish, bake in a quick oven until nicely browned. The more thoroughly it is beaten the better. The same potato is very nice shaped in cones and browned in the oven.

Margery Daw in the Kitchen.

ENTRÉES AND SALADS.

"It is the bounty of nature that we live; but of philosophy, that we eat well." SENECA.

"The Spanish proverb says, that, 'to make a perfect salad there should be a spendthrift for the oil, a miser for the vinegar, a wise man for the salt and mustard, and a madcap to mix them.'"

Potato Salad.

Boil eight medium size potatoes with skins on, when cold, peel and slice them thick. Put on a dressing of salt, pepper, oil and vinegar, and a very little onion.

Mrs. E. R. Booth.

Mayonnaise Dressing.

Yolks of two eggs, one pint of olive oil, one teaspoonful of salt, one teaspoonful of mustard, a pinch of Cayenne pepper. Put yolks and oil in a cool place several hours before using, beat the yolks in a bowl, after beating constantly for five minutes, add salt, mustard and Cayenne pepper, beat thoroughly, then while gently beating, add oil, drop by drop, then in a tiny stream until it begins to thicken, then add the juice of lemon, to thin a little, then the oil until it is consumed. Set on ice till ready for use. Always use a silver fork.

Margery Daw in the Kitchen.

Cheese Soufflé.

Take a cup of grated cheese, one tablespoonful corn starch, one tablespoonful of butter, one cup of milk, four eggs. Put on the milk to boil. When it boils add the corn starch and butter, boil for a few minutes. Beat the yolks of the eggs and pour on the hot mixture. Let it cool and when cold beat the whites and add with the grated cheese. Bake half an hour in a moderate oven. Swiss cheese is best.

Mrs. Wm. T. Booth.

Chocolate Soufflé.

One quarter pound grated vanilla chocolate, one quarter pound almonds blanched and pounded, six ounces sifted sugar, and yolks of eight eggs. Stir this together for a half hour, whisk whites to snow, and stir gently with the rest. Butter mould well, strew it with bread crumbs, put in all and bake one hour.

Mrs. J. J. Halpin.

Lobster Farcie.

Two medium-sized lobsters, one half pint of bread crumbs, one pint cream, one tablespoonful of butter, one and a half tablespoonsful of flour, one half teaspoonful of dry mustard, a dash of red pepper, and salt to taste. Mix these ingredients with a portion of the cream, then add all to the scalding cream and boil one minute. Allow it to cool, then put in small shaped chop dishes or tins, adding bread crumbs and a small lump of butter to each, also a lobster claw pushed in the end, and brown in the oven.

ENTREES AND SALADS.

Purée of Salmon.

Open a small can of salmon and remove all bone, skin, oil, &c. Mash fine. Put over, in a double boiler, one quart of milk, one teaspoonful of salt, one salt spoon ground mace, one pinch of red pepper; add one spoonful of butter and one heaping tablespoonful of corn starch dissolved in a cup of cold water; pour this slowly into boiling milk till it thickens. When smooth and thick, put in salmon. Let cook together five minutes and rub through a fine sieve. Put back and bring to a boil, and eat with crisp crackers (which are Boston crackers, split, buttered, and browned in quick oven).

Welsh Rare-bit.

One pound of cheese cut up in small pieces (fresh country cheese is the best). Put a piece of butter the size of a small egg in a sauce pan, then add the cheese, stir well till nearly melted, then add small teacup of ale, red pepper, salt and mustard to taste. The Rare-bit must be served very hot on buttered toast. This quantity of cheese makes four portions.

Mrs. D. Laurence Shaw.

Hominy Croquettes.

A cup of fresh boiled hominy, a tablespoonful of melted butter, a teaspoonful of sugar, two tablespoonsful of milk, and a well beaten egg. Add enough flour to make into balls, roll in cracker crumbs and fry in hot lard.

St. Andrews M. E. Church Book.

Chicken Soufflé.

For twelve people, the breast of three large chickens is required. Mix one quarter pound of butter with one cup of flour in a sauce pan on the fire, add a pint of milk and beat it up to a smooth sauce. Chop your chicken breast very fine (after boiling) when cold, then mix the sauce thoroughly through it. Add yolks of two eggs, then squeeze it through a sieve.

Beat one pint of cream and whites of two eggs and then mix everything thoroughly together, add salt and juice of the truffles to taste, grease your form, which is better to have a hole in the middle, and put some of the truffles in the bottom, then put mixture in the form, set the mould in a pan of water in a moderate oven with a greased paper on top. Bake from a half to three quarters of an hour. It will rise and when stiff is done.

Mrs. Eva Peterson.

A Nice Way to Cook Chicken.

Cut the chicken up, put into a pan and cover with water; let it stew as usual. When done, make a thickening of cream and flour; add butter, pepper and salt; have ready nice slices of toast cut thick, or shortcake baked, and cut in squares; lay on the dish and pour the chicken and gravy over them while hot.

Broiled Sweetbreads.

Parboil, split, rub well with butter, and broil on a greased gridiron; turn frequently and dip in hot melted butter, to prevent them from getting too dry. Serve with peas.

St. Andrews M. E. Church Book.

Salad Dressing.

Beat the yolks of three eggs with one tablespoonful of sugar, add one half teaspoonful of mustard, one tablespoonful of butter, one teaspoonful of salt, one tumbler of vinegar, set the ingredients in a basin on the range, stirring constantly till it thickens. Add a tablespoonful of sweet cream if you have it.

Margery Daw in the Kitchen.

Chicken Salad.

Take five chickens, boil until very tender leaving them in the liquor to cool. Take them out and cut in small pieces. To one part of chicken take two of celery, but less will do. Cut the celery lengthwise, slice off thin and put in salted ice water until ready to mix.

Dressing.—The yolks of eight or ten raw eggs, one large bottle of salad oil, three or four teaspoonsful of mustard, three teaspoonsful pepper, six teaspoonsful of sugar, one-half cup of vinegar. Beat the yolks until very smooth, then add the oil a few drops at a time, beating all the while. When the oil is half beaten in add the spices, the last half of the oil may be added faster. Just before serving mix the chicken, the celery and nearly all the dressing, reserve a little to pour over the top. Ornament with olives, radishes, &c. This is sufficient for forty persons.

Margery Daw in the Kitchen.

To Roast Birds.

Pluck and draw them, rub a little butter over them, tie a strip of bacon over the breast, and place in a brisk oven for a half hour. Serve with toast and jelly.

Bread Tarts.

Six tablespoonsful of bread crumbs, six tablespoonsful of sugar, six eggs, one wine glass of claret, one pony of brandy, one quarter pound chopped almonds. Chopped citron and lemon rind, two bars of chocolate. Soak bread crumbs in claret and mix all together thoroughly, adding whites of eggs last, well beaten. Serve with or without sauce.

Mrs. J. J. Halpin.

Sidney Smith's Receipt for Salad Dressing.

"Two boiled potatoes, strained through a kitchen sieve,
Softness and smoothness to the salad gives ;
Of mordant mustard take a single spoon,
Distrust the condiment that bites too soon ;
Yet deem it not. Thou man of taste, a fault,
To add a double quantity of salt ;
Four times the spoon with oil of Lucca crown.
And twice with vinegar procured from town;
True taste requires it, and your poet begs
The pounded yellow of two well boiled eggs.
Let onions' atone lurk within bowl,
And, scarce suspected, animate the whole ;
And lastly, in the flavored compound toss
A magic spoonful of anchovy sauce.
Oh, great and glorious ! oh, herbaceous meat!
I would tempt the dying anchorite to eat.
Back to the world he'd turn his weary soul,
And plunge his finger in the salad bowl."

SAUCES.

"Slight flavoring pleases much oftener than much flavoring."

Noodles for Soup.

Take one egg, two tablespoonful of flour, a small teaspoonful of baking powder, a little salt. Beat the egg light, stir the flour with the baking powder and salt, add the egg. Ten minutes before serving the soup, drop this batter from the spoon into it.

Bread Dice for Soup.

Take slices of stale bread cut in small squares; throw into the soup tureen before serving the soup. Crackers crisped in the oven are nice to serve with oyster soup.

Poached Eggs for Consommé.

Break the eggs, which should be very fresh, into a deep sauce-pan half full of boiling water, seasoned with a teaspoonful of salt, and half a gill of vinegar, cover the saucepan, and set it on the back part of the fire until the whites of the eggs are firm, then lift them separately on a skimmer, carefully trim off the rough edges, making each egg a regular oval shape, and slip them off the skimmer into a bowl of hot, but not boiling water, where they must stand for ten minutes before serving.

Egg Balls for Soup.

Rub the yolks of three or four hard boiled eggs to a smooth paste, with a very little melted butter. To this add two raw ones, beaten light, and enough flour to hold the paste together. Make into balls with floured hands, and set in a cold place until just before your soup comes off, when drop in carefully, and boil one minute.

Drawn Butter.

Stir two teaspoonsful of flour into a heaping tablespoonful of butter; stir into a cup of boiling milk, add salt to taste and boil one minute.

Celery Sauce.

Cut up white part of celery, boil well in a very little water, when soft add cream, salt, mace, pepper, flour and butter, mixed together in small quantities.

Miss H.

Creamy Sauce.

Half a cupful of butter, one cupful of powdered sugar, quarter cupful of cream or milk, four tablespoonsful of wine, or one teaspoonsful of lemon or vanilla extract, if lemon or vanilla is used, add four tablespoonsful of cream. Beat the butter to a cream, add sugar gradually, beating all the while. When light and creamy add the wine, and then the cream, a little at a time. When all is beaten smooth, place the basin in a bowl of hot water, and stir until the sauce is smooth and creamy. It will take but a few minutes.

Sauce Tartare.

Two yolks of raw yolks, one half cupful of oil, three tablespoonsful of vinegar, one of mustard, one teaspoonful of sugar, one of salt, one of onion juice, one tablespoonful (each) of chopped capers and chopped cucumber pickles and a little pepper. Make the same as mayonnaise dressing, adding the chopped ingredients last.

Sauce for Plum or Fruit Pudding.

Grate a quarter of a small nutmeg, one cup of sugar, one half cup of butter, one egg (beaten separately), one tablespoon of flour, one third cup of brandy or wine, beat sugar and butter to a cream, add yolk of egg mixed with the flour, then the brandy or wine, and last the white of egg and nutmeg. *Mrs. F. Kellogg.*

BREADS.

*"Dinner may be pleasant,
So may social tea,
But yet, me thinks the breakfast
Is best of all the three."*

In making bread during cold weather, the flour should be thoroughly warmed before mixing. Care should be taken to have the yeast fresh, and to keep the dough from getting chilled while rising.

To Cut Warm Bread.

Heat a thin-bladed knife on the stove or in boiling water.

Tip Top Rolls.

Two heaping cups of flour, one tablespoonful of sugar, one egg, one cup of milk, one tablespoonful of butter, two teaspoonsful of baking powder; bake in roll pan.

Mrs. T. F. Sharpe.

Corn Bread.

One cup of corn meal, one cup of flour, two eggs, two tablespoonsful of melted butter, half a pint of sweet milk, two and a-half teaspoonsful of baking powder, a pinch of salt.

Mrs. T. F. Sharpe.

Tea Rolls.

Two quarts of flour, one pint of milk, one tablespoonful of butter. Scald milk and cool, two dessertspoonsful of sugar, one cup of yeast.

Put all of these in flour, but not mix until morning, then knead and put away to use.

Make into rolls and let rise to bake.

Muffins.

One quart of flour with three teaspoonsful baking powder sifted into it, three eggs, yolks and whites beaten separately, one tablespoonful melted butter, and milk enough for a stiff batter.

Mrs. R. R. Booth.

Puffett.

One pint milk, three pints flour, three teaspoonsful baking powder, three eggs, one tea cup sugar, not quite a cup of butter, a little salt. Bake thirty minutes.

Mrs. F. E. Lathrop.

Biscuits.

One quart flour, three teaspoons baking powder, piece of butter the size of an egg, mix with water, or half milk; roll and cut.

Mrs. F. E. Lathrop.

Muffins.

One quart of milk, three eggs, tablespoonful of butter. Make batter with flour thicker than griddle cakes, two teaspoonsful cream of tartar and one of soda.

Mrs. F. E. Lathrop.

Pop Overs.

Two eggs, two cups milk, two cups flour, piece of butter size of a walnut. Bake in pop-over tins.

Mrs. F. E. Lathrop.

Puffs for Breakfast.

One pint of milk, one pint of flour, two eggs, a piece of butter the size of a egg, a pinch of salt. Place the flour in a basin, make a hollow in the centre, put in the lump of butter, the eggs and the salt. Work butter and eggs well together, and add the milk gradually, bringing all to a smooth batter. Bake in patty pans, from one quarter to half an hour, according to the heat of the oven.

Tea Cakes.

One pint of milk, three eggs, one tablespoon of butter, four large tablespoons of flour, half a teaspoonful of baking powder; bake in jelly cake tins in a quick oven, butter them while hot, and place one above the other.

Waffles.

One quart of sour cream (or milk, and a piece of butter size of an egg) one teaspoonful saluratus, three eggs; make as thick as pancakes, and bake when waffle iron is hot, and well greased.

Corn Bread.

One pint milk, two eggs, one and one half cups flour, two large tablespoonsful melted lard, one teaspoonful of soda, two of cream tartar, salt, and a very little sugar.

Miss Brown.

Corn Cake.

One cup of yellow indian meal, one cup of flour, one egg well beaten separately, one cup of sweet milk, one even teaspoonful of soda, two even teaspoonsful of cream of tartar, a little salt. You can use rye in place of indian for a change.

Mrs. R. R. Booth.

Graham Muffins.

Two cups of graham flour, one half cup of sugar, one cup of milk, one egg, one tablespoonful of butter, two teaspoonsful of Royal Baking Powder, a little salt.

St. Andrew's M. E. Church Book.

Gems.

One cup of flour, one cup of milk, one egg and a little salt. Bake in gem tins about twenty minutes, and serve hot.

DESSERTS.

"Trifles, light as air."

Weights and Measures.

One cup, medium size, holds a half pint.

Two cups, medium size, of sifted flour weighs half a pound.

One pint of sifted flour weighs half a pound.

One pint of sugar weighs one pound.

Two cups of granulated sugar, one pound.

Two tablespoons of liquid, one ounce.

Ten eggs, one pound.

One quart of flour, one pound.

One pint of finely chopped meat, packed solidly, one pound.

Butter, one pint, one pound, when well packed.

A common sized tumbler holds half a pint.

Velvet Cream.

Two tablespoonsful of gelatine dissolved in a half tumbler of water, one pint of rich cream, four tablespoons of sugar, flavor with almond or vanilla extract, or rose water. Put in mould and set on the ice. Serve with whipped cream.

Lemon Cream.

One lemon, peel and juice, four tablespoonsful of sugar, two tablespoonsful cold water. Beat the yolks of four eggs, and add the lemon, sugar and water ; let it thicken on the stove, stirring constantly, then stir in the beaten whites of the eggs with two tablespoons of sugar, and take the mixture off the fire.

Margery Daw in the Kitchen.

Huckleberry Pudding.

One quart of canned huckleberries, one quart of flour, one pint molasses, one tablespoon of soda. Mix molasses well together. Put some of the flour on the berries, mix all together, adding spice, cinnamon, allspice, ginger, in all a tablespoonful. A very little cloves, mace, and add salt. Steam three hours.

Mrs. G. Hickok.

Cream Pie.

Six eggs, two cups of sugar, two cups flour, one teaspoonful of soda ; two of cream tartar. Beat eggs separately; then together, add sugar, then soda dissolved in water and cream tartar mixed in flour, then add flour. Bake in jelly cake pans.

CUSTARD FOR SAUCE.—Two eggs, one cup sugar, three-quarters of a cup of flour (or corn starch), one pint of milk. This is put between two loaves of cake (as jelly cake) with or without a meringue on top, and one half teaspoonful of vanilla. This makes three loaves, and two eggs makes a meringue for one pie.

Cold Cream Pudding.

One pound of loaf sugar, quarter of a pint of water, boiled together until the sugar begins to rope, the whites of eight eggs, beaten to a stiff froth ; mix these with the above while hot; one quarter of a box of gelatine, dissolved in a little water, add a little peach juice (either canned or fresh), three peaches sliced fine, some pineapple and oranges, a little grated cocoanut; flavor with vanilla, liquid sauce, with a little orange juice, and grated rind.

Ambrosia.

Sliced oranges and grated cocoanut laid in layers in a glass dish, and serve.

Mrs. F. Kellogg.

Coffee Jelly.

One pint of sugar, one pint of strong coffee, a pint and a half of boiling water, half a pint of cold water, a box of gelatine. Soak the gelatine two hours in the cold water, pour the boiling water on it, and when it is dissolved add the sugar and coffee, strain. turn into moulds, and set away to harden; to be served with sugar and cream.

Miss Parloa.

Caramel Custard.

Two heaping tablespoonsful dark brown sugar, burn in an old tin, mix with enough milk to soften it. Then strain it, and stir it into a quart of soft custard. Flavor with vanilla.

Mrs. F. E. Lathrop.

Wine Jelly.

One box of gelatine in a pint of cold water, with the juice, and grated peel of three lemons. Let this stand overnight, then add one quart of boiling water, one pound of granulated sugar, one pint of sherry or white wine, stir until it is dissolved, and strain through paper muslin, then pour into moulds or tumblers, and stand in a cool place until hard.

Mrs. W. H. Beadleston.

Indian Pudding.

One quart of milk and a little salt, with one quarter pound suet, finely chopped. Let them be scalding hot, put the dish in a kettle of boiling water to avoid burning, and add a little nutmeg, indian meal, to make it of the consistency of mush, sweeten to taste (two scant cups of meal stirred in gradually).

Mrs F. E. Lathrop.

Pie Pastry.

Three cups of flour, one cup of lard, and almost a cup of water, mix together with knife, roll thin and spread with very little butter, the second rolling use for crust.

Mrs. F. E. Lathrop.

Lemon and Raisin Pie.

Take the inside of one lemon, except the seeds, chop with half a cupful of seeded raisins, add two small tablespoonsful of flour, one cup of sugar, and one cup of water; bake with two crusts. This makes one pie.

Berkshire Cook Book.

Fig Pudding.

One half pound bread crumbs, one half pound of figs, one half pound of brown sugar, two eggs, a little nutmeg, one quarter pound suet, a teacup of milk, one quarter pound of flour. The figs and suet to be chopped very fine and mixed with the bread crumbs, flour, sugar and nutmeg; stir all together and add the milk and eggs well beaten. Boil in a mould four hours. To be eaten with sauce, hard or soft.

Mrs. W. H. Beadleston.

Lemon Pudding.

Beat together the yolks of ten eggs, one half pound of powdered sugar, juice of three lemons and peel of one. Soak one ounce of gelatine in three-eights of a pint of hot water, and beat well. Beat whites of eggs very stiff and stir in last.

Sauce.—Boil one pint of cream, and one quarter of a pound of powdered sugar. Beat yolks of four eggs, and stir in, flavor to taste.

Norwegian Recipe. Mrs. Donald.

Orange Baskets.

Make baskets of eight oranges, strain the juice and make a jelly, with three pints of water, gelatine and sugar. Fill baskets, and when firm, cut orange peel in quarters, tie with ribbon, and serve one on each plate, with whips, made with cream to ornament the top.

Mrs. J. J. Halpin.

Raspberry Joy.

Take the juice from a can of raspberries and strain it, then beat to a froth the whites of four eggs, adding a cup of powdered sugar, gradually stir in the juice and a teaspoonful of gelatine dissolved in a half teacup of water; pour in moulds and freeze before serving.

Mrs. J. J. Halpin.

CAKE.

*" With weights and measures just and true,
Oven of even heat,
Well buttered tins and quiet nerves,
Success will be complete."*

General Directions.

FLOUR.—Should always be sifted before using.

CREAM OF TARTAR—or baking powder should be sifted in the flour.

SODA.—Should always be dissolved in the milk.

BUTTER AND SUGAR.—For cake, should always be beaten to a cream.

EGGS.—Beat the yolks until you can take up a spoonful; whip the whites to a stiff froth, and stir them into the cake with the flour, the last thing before putting the cake into tins.

TO BOIL A PUDDING.—Dip the bag into cold water, and sprinkle the inside with flour.

TO PREVENT THE JUICE FROM RUNNING OUT OF A PIE. — Take a a strip of muslin wide enough to cover the edge of the pie and go around it and lap ; wet the cloth in cold water, and pin around the pie; when it is taken from the oven, remove the cloth.

Delicate Cake.

Two cups of sugar (granulated), one cup of butter, two cups of flour, one cup of milk, one cup of corn starch; the whites of six eggs, two teaspoonsful of baking powder, mix sugar and butter to a cream, then take half of the milk and mix with sugar and butter, and sift flour twice: mix corn starch with the remainder of milk, and at the last, mix the eggs beaten to a stiff froth. Soft icing flavored with lemon.

Mrs. G. Hickok.

Angel Cake.

One cup of flour, one and one half cups of powdered sugar, one teaspoonful of cream tartar mixed with flour sifted twelve times. Whites of eleven eggs beaten to a stiff froth, one teaspoonful of vanilla, then beat more. Stir the flour and sugar in egg sufficient to mix. Do not grease the tin. Bake thirty of forty minutes in a slow oven. When taken out of the oven, turn in a colander upside down.

Mrs. F. Kellogg.

Coffee Cake.

One scant cup of granulated sugar, two thirds of a cup of butter, two eggs, two cups of flour, two teaspoonsful of baking powder, two thirds cake of Baker's chocolate dissolved in one cup of boiling hot coffee, strong flavor.

SOFT ICING.—One cup sugar, one third cup of boiling water. Boil five minutes without stirring, then stir until it hardens.

Mrs. G. Hickok.

Helen Cake.

Two cups of sugar, half a cup butter, three cups of flour, one cup of sweet milk, three eggs, two teaspoonful of baking powder. Bake in square tins, sprinkle half cup stifted sugar on the top before baking.

Mrs. T. F. Sharpe.

Crullers.

Two and a half cups powdered sugar, one half cup butter one pint milk, three eggs, two teaspoonsful of soda, three teaspoonsful cream tartar, a little salt, nutmeg and lemon flavor, mix soft. Cut in fancy shapes and fry in hot lard.

Miss Beadleston.

Orange Cake.

Two cups of sugar, two cups of flour, half a cup of water that has been boiled and cooled, yolks of five eggs, whites of four eggs, the rind and juice of one sour orange, half a teaspoon of soda, one teaspoonful of cream of tartar ; bake in layers. Take the rind and juice of one orange, the white of one egg, beaten to a stiff froth, sugar enough to stiffen, spread between the layers, and on top.

Molasses Cake.

Two cups of molasses, one cup of butter mixed together, one tablespoonful of soda dissolved in one cup of boiling water, stir quickly and thicken with flour, adding one half teaspoonful of essence of lemon and one half teaspoonful vanilla. Dried currants or raisins make it a delicious cake, or spices may be added if desired.

Mrs. A. Hay.

Sponge Cake.

Beat four eggs very light, yolks and whites together, then beat in two cups of powdered sugar, one cup of sifted flour, a little at a time, then a second cup of flour, with two teaspoonsful of baking powder mixed in it, the juice and rind of one lemon, lastly a small tea cup full of almost boiling water stirred in gradually, put in a moderate oven and do not look at it for twenty minutes. It should be done in that time. Do not stir sponge cake from the bottom when adding the last flour, or it will be heavy.

Mrs. A. Hay.

Orange Cake.

Five eggs beaten separately, three coffee cups of sugar, three quarters of a coffee cup of butter, one coffee cup of sweet milk, four coffee cups of flour, juice of one orange, and a little of the rind (grated), one teaspoonful of soda, two teaspoonsful of cream of tartar. Place yolks, sugar, butter, and the orange juice in a large bowl; beat until light and creamy. Then add the milk, whites of eggs, beaten to a stiff froth, then the flour (soda and saleratus); dissolve soda in the milk. Bake in jelly pans.

Icing.—One coffee cup of granulated sugar, white of one egg, juice of one orange. Put the sugar on stove, in just enough water to moisten; let it boil until clear, and will spin a thread. Have the whites of the egg well beaten, and have some one drip the sugar in while you are beating, and continue to beat until it is thick and white, then stir in the orange juice; should it make it too thin, add more sugar until thick enough. This makes a very large and delicious cake.

Mrs. F. Kellogg.

Pearl Cake.

Two cups of sugar, one half cup of butter, one cup sweet milk, three and a half cups of sifted flour, one third cup corn starch, whites of five eggs, two teaspoonsful of cream tartar and one of soda, or three of baking powder.

Mrs. A. Hay.

Ginger Cake.

One cup milk, one cup molasses, very large tablespoon of drippings, one egg, one quarter teaspoonful of soda, cinnamon, ginger and not very thick with flour, and a little salt.

Miss H.

Jumbles.

One pound sugar, not quite a pound of butter, three eggs, a little grated nutmeg, a small quantity of soda in a half cup of milk, or less, to dissolve it, but not enough to thin the mixture too much, roll out as thin as possible and cut.

Miss H.

Fig Cake.

One cup of pulverized sugar, one half cup of butter, one cup of milk, three cups of flour, yolks of three eggs. Reserve the whites for filling. Two teapoonsful (even) of baking powder, in the sifted flour. Bake in jelly cake tins.

FILLING.—Boil one coffee cup of granulated sugar with a tablespoonful of water in a porcelain sauce pan till it drops like candy in cold water. Have the whites of the eggs beaten stiff, and pour the boiling icing into whites, and add the figs after. Have a half-pound of figs boiled one hour and chopped fine, then add all together and put between the layers.

Mrs. Varick.

Sponge Cake.

One pound sugar, ten eggs, half pound flour and one lemon. Beat eggs separately, and add juice and grated rind of a large lemon, beat well before putting flour in, which comes last.

Mrs. F. E. Lathrop.

Bread Cake.

Two cups of dough, one cup of sugar, one half cup of butter, two eggs, one half tablespoonful of milk, one half teaspoonful soda dissolved in the milk, one half cup of raisins, one half cup of currants; add cinnamon, cloves, and nutmeg to taste. Let raise for some time, the longer the better, and bake in not too hot an oven, until thoroughly done.

Miss R. H.

CANDIES.

WITHOUT COOKING.

"Sweets to the Sweet."

French Cream.

These candies are made without boiling, which makes them very desirable, and they are equal to the best French creams. The secret lies in the sugar used which is the XXX powdered or confectioners sugar. It can be obtained at the large groceries. Ordinary powdered sugar when rubbed between the thumb and finger has a decided grain, but the confectioners sugar is fine as flour. Margery Daw promises perfect success in following these recipes.

French Vanilla Cream.

Break into a bowl the white of one or more eggs, as the quantity you wish to make will require, add to it an equal quantity of cold water, then stir in XXX powdered or confectioners' sugar until you have it stiff enough to mould into shape with the fingers. Flavor with vanilla to taste. After it is formed into balls, cubes or lozenger shapes, lay them upon plates or waxed paper and set them aside to dry. This cream is the foundation of all French creams.

English Walnut Creams.

Make French cream as previously directed. Have ready some English walnuts, using care not to break the meats. Make a ball of the cream about the size of a walnut and place a half nut meat upon either side of the ball, pressing it into the cream. Lay them away for a few hours to dry.

Cream Cherries.

Make a small round ball of French cream, cut a strip of citron the size of a cherry stem, and put the ball of cream upon one end of it. Take a cherry glacé, and cutting it in two, put one half each side of the stem on the cream ball and it will make a very pretty candy. They can also be made like walnut creams, using cherries instead of walnuts.
Margery Daw in the Kitchen.

Cream Dates.

Select perfect dates, and with a knife remove the pit. Take a piece of French cream, make an oblong shape, and wrap the date around the cream.

Wintergreen Creams.

Make the cream as directed for French cream, flavor with wintergreen essence to taste. Color pink with cochineal syrup, and form into round lozenger shapes.
Margery Daw in the Kitchen.

Peppermint Creams.

Make the cream as directed for French creams, flavoring it quite strong with essence of peppermint. Take small bits of the cream and shape into round flat forms.

Maple Sugar Creams.

Grate maple sugar, mix it in quantities to suit taste, with French cream, adding enough confectioners sugar to mould into any shape desired. Walnut creams are sometimes made with maple sugar and are very nice.

CANDIES.

COOKED.

Molasses Taffy.

One cup of molasses, one cup of sugar, a piece of butter the size of an egg. Boil hard, and test in cold water; when brittle, pour in thin cakes on buttered tins; as it cools mark in squares with the back of a knife.

Margery Daw in the Kitchen.

Pea-nut Candy.

Two cups molasses, one cup of brown sugar, one tablespoonful of butter and one of vinegar. Put into a kettle to boil. Having cracked and rubbed the skin from the pea-nuts, put them into buttered pans, and when the candy is done pour it over the nuts. Cut into blocks while warm.

Chocolate Caramels.

One cup sugar, one cup molasses, one cup of chocolate, one half cup of milk, a piece of butter size of an egg. Test in water before putting in the grated chocolate, if it hardens, add the chocolate, and cook only a short time, then pour into buttered pans. When cool mark into blocks with the back of a knife.

Miss H.

Molasses Candy.

Two cups of molasses, one cup of sugar, a piece of butter the size of a small egg, one tablespoonful of glycerine. Put these ingredients into a kettle and boil hard twenty or thirty minutes. When boiled thick drop a few drops in a cup of cold water, and if the drops retain their shape it is nearly done, which will be when it is brittle; do not boil it too much. Have pans or platters well buttered, and just before the candy is poured into them, stir in one half teaspoonful of cream tartar or soda. If flavoring is desired, drop the flavoring on the top as it begins to cool, and when it is pulled the whole will be flavored. Pull till as white as desired, and draw into sticks and cut with shears.

Everton Taffy.

Three pounds of brown sugar, one and one half pints of water, not quite half a pound of butter. Boil until the syrup becomes crisp.

Chocolate Creams.

Use French cream and form it into small cone-shaped balls with the fingers; lay them upon oiled paper to harden until all are formed. Melt one cake of baker's chocolate in an earthen dish or small basin; by setting it in the oven it will soon melt; do not let it cook. To keep the chocolate hot, it is well to have a hot soap stone, and place the basin with the chocolate upon it. Take the balls of cream one at a time on a silver fork, pour the melted chocolate over them with a teaspoon and slip them from the fork upon oiled paper.

Butter Scotch.

One cup of brown sugar, one half cup of water, one teaspoonful of vinegar, piece of butter the size of a walnut. Boil about twenty minutes, flavor if desired.

Margery Daw in the Kitchen.

Pea-nut Candy.

Shell your peanuts and chop them fine; measure them in a cup, and take just the same quantity of granulated sugar as you have peanuts. Put the sugar in a skillet or spider, on the fire, and keep moving the skillet around until the sugar is dissolved; then put in the peanuts and pour into buttered tins. This is delicious and so quickly made.

Miss B.

Pop Corn Balls.

Six quarts of popped corn, one pint of molasses. Boil the molasses about fifteen minutes; then put the corn into a large pan, pour the molasses over it, and stir briskly until thoroughly mixed. Then, with clean hands, make into balls of the desired size, or put in buttered pans.

HINTS FOR THE SICK.

Never keep fruit in a sick room; the sight of it is apt to lessen the appetite for it. An orange delicately prepared, or a bunch of Malaga or other nice grapes, brought in on a dessert plate with a few green leaves, will form a tempting and agreeable surprise to the capricious appetite of an invalid.

Sago, prepared like a custard, then baked with apples is an excellent sick room pudding.

Oysters are good for the sick, especially raw (without vinegar, lemon juice may be used) a very few at a time. They are easily digested and agreeable to the palate.

Fresh tea should be made as often as the invalid needs it, and no food nor drink should remain in the sick room but should be kept in adjoining room or outside of the window where they would be fresh and cool.

Every meal should be a surprise, and the patient should be left alone while eating if possible.

Food should be made as attractive as possible, served in the choicest china, with the cleanest of napkins and the brightest of silver.

Beef Tea.

Take one pound of lean beef, chopped fine (at the market) pour over it one pint of cold water, let it stand an hour. Then set it on the back of the range, and let it simmer slowly about three quarters of an hour; strain and salt when used.

Chicken Broth.

One chicken jointed, cover it with water, and let it boil, closely covered, until the meat drops from the bones. Skim off the fat, strain and season with salt, and if desired a teaspoonful or two of rice, and let it boil until the rice is cooked. In some cases of nausea a cup of chicken broth will prove efficacious.

Mutton Broth.

To each pound of meat add one quart of cold water, bring gently to a boil, skim it and salt to taste ; simmer three hours. A teaspoonful or more of rice may be added, and boil till the rice is cooked.

Oatmeal Gruel.

Stir two large spoonsful of oatmeal into one pint of boiling water, boil gently one half hour, skim, and add a little salt, sugar and nutmeg.

Lemonade.

Two large juicy lemons, or three smaller ones, one large cup of sugar, and one quart of ice water. Ripe strawberries mashed and added are very delicious, or grated pine apple if preferred.

Flaxseed Tea.

One half pound of flaxseed, one half pound of rock candy, the juice of three lemons, the skin may be cut into small pieces and added. Pour over this two quarts of boiling water, and let it stand until perfectly cold. Strain before drinking; this is good for a cough; more sugar and lemon may be added.

Cure for a Felon.

Two drachms of gum ammoniac dissolved in one ounce of alcohol. Bind the finger up in a linen cloth, and keep it constantly wet with the solution. Add more alcohol if necessary. (Gum ammoniac is a brown gum). This has been tried very successfully.

To Check a Cold.

As soon as you feel that you have taken cold, fill a glass half full of water, drop into it six drops of spirits of camphor, stir it and take a dessertspoonful every twenty minutes. This is remarkably successful if taken according to directions.

Koumys.

Three pints of milk, one tablespoonful of sugar, one half Viennese yeast cake. Place on stove and let it grow warm very slowly, a little over blood heat, one hundred degrees. Take milk and strain it and bottle, placing bottles near fire and heat through turning bottles every ten minutes. After shaking put in window till cool, then put in ice box. Heat bottles before filling with koumys; use bottles with fastenings like beer bottles.

Mrs. J. J. Halpin.

Koumys.

One quart of milk, one dessertspoonful of brewers yeast, one teaspoonful sugar, mix last two together and a little milk, then stir thoroughly into the rest of the milk and bottle. After bottling keep in warm room for twelve hours, then put in a cold place and the second or third day it will be ready for use.

Miss H.

For Catarrh.

Pulverized camphor, carbonate of soda, powdered sugar, half as much sugar as camphor, half as much soda as sugar. Mix thoroughly in a mortar and snuff half hour before retiring, also in morning when arising.

Miss H.

Rheumatism or any Pain.

One tablespoon of laudanum, one teaspoon baking soda, half pint of water; heat all together, and wring out a flannel in it, and apply as hot as possible.

Miss H.

Throat Gargle.

One pint hot water, one tablespoon of tannin, two tablespoonsful glycerine, gargle often, excellent for sore throat.

Miss H.

Tonic.

Thirty grains of quinine in one pint of sherry, with forty drops of diluted sulphuric acid to mix the two.

Miss H.

Cough Mixture.

One ounce horehound, one ounce hops, one ounce boneset, one quarter pound gum arabic. Steep herbs in one quart boiling water several hours, then add gum arabic, and sugar to taste; boil until rather thick, strain and bottle and keep in a cool place, add a little liquor before bottling, so that it will not sour. Six or seven teaspoonsful a day or more, if cough is troublesome.

Miss H.

Hoarseness.

Lemon juice, gum arabic and rock candy, or loaf sugar, a tablespoonful of the solids, and juice of half a lemon. Take a little at a time.

Excellent Tonic.

Three ounces wild cherry bark (chips), one quart old Jamaica rum, two quarts cold water, three-quarters pound granulated sugar. Soak the bark in cold water forty-eight hours, then strain off till perfectly clear. Add one quart of best old rum, then the sugar, stir well and allow it to stand a few minutes. Then stir again, and pour into bottles; cork tightly.

Miss Adams.

Chalk Mixture.

To be taken in cases of diarrhœa as a relief or help, but not depended on entirely as a cure. Take two sticks of cinnamon and steep them, add a little sugar and strain. For a coffee cup full of cinnamon put about two teaspoonsful of chalk. Take a teaspoonful several times a a day.

ODDS AND ENDS.

For Cleaning Brass.

Make a thin paste of plate powder, two tablespoonsful of vinegar, four tablespoonsful of alcohol; rub on with a piece flannel; polish with chamois.

Baking Custard.

A satisfactory way to cook custard is to put the pudding dish or cups containing the mixture in a pan of hot water, in a moderately hot oven. This will prevent the custard from getting watery.

Tooth Powder.

One fourth of a pound precipated chalk, one-fourth of a pound of pulvarized orris root, one ounce of pulverized sugar; mix all together, and flavor with wintergreen.

To Freshen Black Lace.

Put in a bowl or tumbler equal quantities of water and alcohol, let the lace lay in it a minute, then squeeze it out well, and pin out smooth on a newspaper to dry, and you will find your lace equal to new.

Mrs. Lathrop.

Celery.

Roll celery in brown paper and then in cloth, put in dry place, and it will keep a week.

Remove Ink from Carpets.

First take up as much as possible of the ink with a teaspoon, then pour cold milk upon the spot, and take up as before, pouring on milk until at last it becomes only slightly tinged with black; then wash with cold water, and absorb with a cloth, without too much rubbing.

To Polish Furniture.

One cup of alcohol, one cup of turpentine, and two cups of sweet oil.

A little soap put on the hinges or latch of a door will stop its creaking.

If brooms were given a hot bath once a week they would last longer, and retain their shape until nearly worn out.

A Poetical Appetizer.

"Always have lobster sauce with salmon,
And put mint sauce your roasted lamb on.

Veal cutlet dip in egg and bread crumbs,
Fry till you see a brownish red come.

In dressing salad mind this law;
With two hard yolks use one that's raw.

Roast pork, *sans* apple sauce, past doubt,
Is Hamlet with the Prince left out.

Broil lightly your beefsteak—to fry it
Argues contempt of Christian diet.

To roast spring chickens is to spoil 'em,
Just split 'em down the back and broil 'em.

It gives true epicures the vapors
To see boiled mutton minus capers.

The cook deserves a hearty cuffing
Who serves roast fowl with tasteless stuffing.

Nice oyster sauce gives zest to cod—
A fish when fresh to feast a god.

But we might rhyme for weeks this way,
And still have lots of things to say."

—*Selected.*

Cary & Moen Co.,

Manufacturers of Steel Wire for all Purposes and Steel Springs

OF EVERY DESCRIPTION.

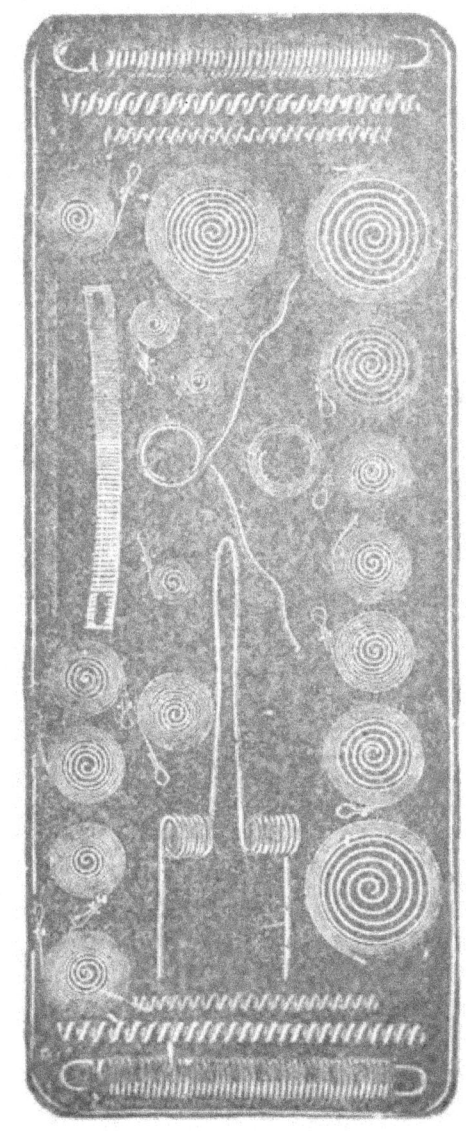

MARKET STEEL WIRE.

Also Patent Tempered Steel Furniture Springs Constantly on Hand.

WORKS: 232 to 238 W. 29th St, 225 to 229 W. 28th St. OFFICE: 234 W. 29th St.

NEW YORK.

PRIDE OF THE WEST.

Special attention is called to the celebrated brand of

Bleached ✻ Muslin,

which for

Fineness and Durability is Unsurpassed.

This cloth is manufactured with great care, particularly for **LADIES' USE**, in 36, 40, and 45-inch widths, and is guaranteed not to crack or turn yellow. *Inquire for this brand and take no substitute.*

For sale by all leading retail dry goods dealers in the United States.

Established in New York 1836.

H. A. CASSEBEER,

APOTHECARY,

1176 NINTH AVENUE.   **292 SIXTH AVENUE.**
Corner 72d St.   Bet. 18th & 19th Sts.

Doctors Prescriptions and Family Receipts Carefully and Accurately Prepared.

WILLIAM H. GRAY,

ESTABLISHED 1850.

20 & 22 WOOSTER ST.

Manufacturer
Importer   IN   Fine Carriages.
Dealer

Victorias, T Carts, Cabriolets, Stanhope Phaetons, Broughams, Spider Phaetons, Wagonettes, Landaus, Two Wheelers.

FOUR - IN - HAND TRAPS.

NATURAL ∴ WOOD ∴ VEHICLES

In Every Conceivable Shape.

The largest and most complete assortment in the City at exceedingly moderate prices.

LOUIS F. MAZZETTI
CATERER
AND
Confectioner.

Large and Magnificent Banquet Hall for Receptions, Weddings and Sociables. Also smaller rooms for Committees, Re-unions, etc.

Main Store, 49th St. and 6th Avenue.
Telephone Call, 402-39th.

Branches: { 74th St. & 9th Ave.,   Telephone, 1159-39th
           { 44 West 125th St.,   " 152 Harlem

WEST END MARKET.

Joseph Schuler,
CHOICE MEATS,
Philadelphia Poultry and Game.

282 GRAND BOULEVARD,   Bet. 73d and 74th Sts.

Silver King Spice Mills.

D. Lawrence Shaw,
PROPRIETOR.

74 Warren Street,
NEW YORK.

Importer and Manufacturer

OF

SPICES, MUSTARDS,

AND

BAKING POWDERS.

LORING MARKET.

CHAS. MAYER,

Dealer in Choice

Beef, Veal, Mutton, Lamb, Pork, &c.,

Poultry and Game in Season.

Also Fish, Oysters and Clams Constantly on hand.

1188 TENTH AVENUE,

Southeast Corner 73d Street,   NEW YORK.

GEORGE H. TIEMEYER,

Dealer in

Staple & Fancy Groceries,

Importer of

WINES, LIQUORS & SEGARS,

FANCY FRUITS AND VEGETABLES.

1190 and 1192 Tenth Avenue,

Corner 73d Street,   NEW YORK.

SAMUEL F. ADAMS,
Counselor at Law.

WM. CRITTENDEN ADAMS.
Commissioner of Deeds.

Adams Bros.,
Real Estate Brokers,
432 Fifth Avenue,
New York City.

Personal Attention given to the Management of Estates.

Mrs. J. R. DeNike,

456 East 120th Street,

New York.

Mrs. DeNike would call especial attention to her Hair Tonic, which she has used successfully for over ten years. It is prepared in the most careful manner from herbs, contains no oil, and is warranted to remove dandruff, prevent the hair from falling out, and cause hair to grow on bald spots if they are not perfectly smooth.

Refers to Mrs. Robert Russell Booth.

FREDERICK VAGTS,

DEALER IN

Fancy - and - Staple - Groceries,

TEAS AND WINES,

NINTH AVENUE & 83D STREET.

WOOD & RADIKER.

GROCERS.

We beg to call the attention of our numerous friends and patrons to the above change of name in the business carried on at this address. Trusting to receive a continuance of your esteemed orders.

Respectfully,

WOOD & RADIKER,

1402 NINTH AVENUE,   Cor. 83d Street.

Jaeger's Confectionery.

Madison Ave., cor. 59th Street.

Branch: Ninth Avenue, cor. 72d Street.

Horton's Ice Cream,

MADE FROM PURE CREAM.

Horton's Super Frozen Bricks of Ice Cream for Church Fairs, etc., a Specialty.

DEPOTS:

1219 Ninth Avenue.   142 West 125th Street.

598 Sixth Avenue, and 305 Fourth Avenue.

English Enamel.

The Best in the Market.

Ready for Use, in Self-Opening Tins.

150 Tints, Exquisite Colors, Surface like Porcelain. Can be Applied by Anyone.

11 PRIZE MEDALS.

INVENTED BY

Thomas Griffiths, F.C.S., M.S.A.,

Original Inventor of Enamel Paint, for Renovating and Decorating Anthing and Everything.

Furniture, Metal Ware, Wicker Work, Fans, Water Cans.

25 & 50 Cents. by the Gallon to Decorators,

Etc., Etc.

Send for Tint Cards.

'VITROS' BATH ENAMEL

60 Cents and $1.

English Enamel Paint Co.,

10 EAST 15TH STREET,

NEW YORK.

D. E. DEMAREST,

Successor to **MRS. W. MILLES.**

DEALER IN NOTIONS, FANCY GOODS,

Ladies and Gent's Furnishings,

1213 NINTH AVENUE,

Second door from 74th St.

Agent for the "Staten Island" Cleaning and Dyeing Establishment, and the "Troy" Steam Laundry.

T. C. CAMPBELL,

329 WEST BOULEVARD, Cor. 76th St.

DEALER IN

DRY & FANCY GOODS,

PERFUMERY, POCKET KNIVES & SCISSORS,

Home and Foreign Weekly and Monthly Magazines.

Agent for TROY LAUNDRY CO.

West End School,

115 West 71st Street.

Collegiate, Junior and Primary
DEPARTMENTS.

New Gymnasium, Military Drill.

Chester Donaldson, A.M.,
Head Master.

The Hudson River Bank,

OF THE CITY OF NEW YORK.

Ninth Avenue, Cor. 72d Street.

Capital, - - 200,000.   Surplus, - - 100,000.

—◆— OFFICERS. —◆—

PRESIDENT,
W. De Groot.

VICE-PRESIDENT,
Charles L. Acker.

CASHIER,
Peter Snyder.

BOEDECKER,

9TH AVE. AND 72D ST.

3d Ave. & 63d Street. | 7th Ave. & 122d Street.

CLEANSING, DYEING,

Renovating and Refinishing.

Fine French Laundry Work.

REFINISHING.

Laces and Lace Curtains a Specialty.

H. Lahnstein,

CAMBRIDGE ✢ MARKET,

1404 Ninth Avenue,

Bet. 83d & 84th Sts.,   NEW YORK.

Choice Meats and Poultry.   Vegetables, Fish and Oysters.
Game in Season.

Thomas Dimond.   J. G. Dimond, Jr.

ESTABLISHED 1852.

J. G. & T. DIMOND,

ARCHITECTURAL

IRON WORKS,

209 & 211 W. 33d Street,

NEW YORK.

All kinds of Iron Work for Buildings.

Telephone Call, 39th St., 298.

JACOB WINKLER'S.

HAMILTON

Meat and Vegetable Market,

1386 NINTH AVE.,

Bet. 82d and 83d Sts.,   NEW YORK.

Orders received for Fish and Oysters.

Telephone Call, 894 39th St.

JOHN A. KELLY,

Dakota Livery Stables,

75TH ST., BOULEVARD & TENTH AVENUE,

NEW YORK.

Branch Office, 1463 Ninth Avenue.

Coaches, Coupes, Landaus, Victorias and Light Wagons, Always in Readiness.

CHARLES T. WILLS,

BUILDER,

10 WEST 23D STREET.

Mrs. Eva Peterson,

Cook for Dinner, Parties & Luncheons.

No. 670 SIXTH AVENUE.

New York.

Refer to Mrs. F. F. Lathrop.

J. THODE,
UPHOLSTERER AND CABINET MAKER.

Furniture Recovered, Varnished, etc. Carpets cleaned by steam, refitted and laid. Spring Hair Mattresses and Pillows made over.

307 GRAND BOULEVARD,

Between 74th and 75th Sts.   NEW YORK.

VAGTS & HEITMANN,

Dealers in

FINE GROCERIES,

Teas, Wines, Liquors and Cigars,

Fruits and Vegetables.

284 Western Boulevard,

Cor. 74th Street,   NEW YORK.

Branch of 1397 9th Ave., cor. 83d Street.

ESTABLISHED, 1834.   INCORPORATED, 1874.

NOTICE.

THE ALLAN HAY CO.'S
OFFICE

REMOVED FROM
306 - FOURTH - AVENUE,
TO
Works : 621 West 38th Street.

James L. Libby.   Edward W. Scott, Jr.   Walter E. Scott.

LIBBY & SCOTT BROS.,
REAL ESTATE & LOANS,
EQUITABLE BUILDING,

120 BROADWAY.

Nassau St. Entrance.   NEW YORK.

Charles Otten.   Henry A. Flagge

OTTEN & FLAGGE,

Grocers,

73d Street and 9th Avenue,

NEW YORK.

www.ingramcontent.com/pod-product-compliance
Lightning Source LLC
Chambersburg PA
CBHW031347160426
43196CB00007B/760